Christmas Carols

Illustrated by

Sandy Nightingale

MACMILLAN CHILDR

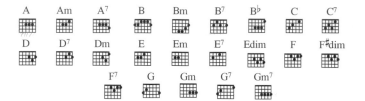

GUITAR CHORDS

First published 1988 by Macmillan Children's Books

This edition published 2005 by Macmillan Children's Books
a division of Macmillan Publishers Limited
20 New Wharf Road, London N1 9RR Basingstoke and Oxford
www.panmacmillan.com

Associated companies throughout the world

ISBN 0 330 43978 2

This collection copyright © Macmillan Children's Books 1988
Illustrations copyright © Sandy Nightingale 1988
Music setting copyright © Lucy Duke 1988
Music processed by Halstan & Co. Ltd., Amersham, Bucks., England

1 3 5 7 9 8 6 4 2

A CIP catalogue record for this book is available from the British Library.

Music processed by Halstan & Co. Ltd., Amersham, Bucks., England
Printed in China

Contents

We Wish You a Merry Christmas

1. We wish you a mer - ry

Christ - mas, We wish you a mer - ry

Christ - mas, We wish you a mer - ry

Christ - mas, And a hap - py New Year.

CHORUS

Good ti - dings we bring To

you and your kin, We wish you a mer - ry

Christ- mas, And a   hap - py New   Year.

2. Now bring us some figgy pudding,
   Now bring us some figgy pudding,
   Now bring us some figgy pudding,
   And bring some out here.
       Good tidings we bring
       To you and your kin,
       We wish you a merry Christmas,
       And a happy New Year.

3. For we all like figgy pudding,
   For we all like figgy pudding,
   For we all like figgy pudding,
   So bring some out here.
       Good tidings we bring
       To you and your kin,
       We wish you a merry Christmas,
       And a happy New Year.

4. And we won't go until we've had some,
   And we won't go until we've had some,
   And we won't go until we've had some,
   So bring some out here.
      Good tidings we bring
      To you and your kin,
      We wish you a merry Christmas,
      And a happy New Year.

It Came upon a Midnight Clear

1. It____ came up - on a____ mid - night clear That glo - rious song of old, From an - gels bend - ing near the earth To__ touch their harps of gold: 'Peace on the earth, good will to men, From

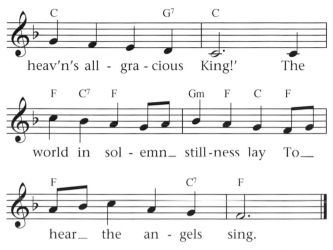

heav'n's all - gra - cious King!' The
world in sol - emn_ still-ness lay To_
hear_ the an - gels sing.

2. Still through the cloven skies they come,
   With peaceful wings unfurled;
   And still their heavenly music floats
   O'er all the weary world:
   Above its sad and lowly plains
   They bend on hovering wing;
   And ever o'er its Babel-sounds
   The blessèd angels sing.

3. Yet with the woes of sin and strife
   The world has suffered long;
   Beneath the angel-strain have rolled
   Two thousand years of wrong;
   And man, at war with man, hears not
   The love-song which they bring:
   O hush the noise, ye men of strife,
   And hear the angels sing.

4. And ye, beneath life's crushing load,
   Whose forms are bending low,
   Who toil along the climbing way
   With painful steps and slow,
   Look now! for glad and golden hours
   Come swiftly on the wing;
   O rest beside the weary road,
   And hear the angels sing.

5. For lo, the days are hastening on,
   By prophet-bards foretold,
   When, with the ever-circling years,
   Comes round the age of gold;
   When peace shall over all the earth
   Its ancient splendours fling,
   And the whole world give back the song
   Which now the angels sing.

Good King Wenceslas

1. Good King Wen - ces - las looked out,

On the feast of Steph - en,

When the snow lay round a - bout,

Deep and crisp and ev - en:

Bright - ly shone the moon that night,

Though the frost was cru - el,

When a poor man came in sight,

Gath -'ring win -ter fu - el.

2. 'Hither page and stand by me,
   If thou knowest it, telling,
   Yonder peasant who is he?
   Where and what his dwelling?'
   'Sire, he lives a good league hence,
   Underneath the mountain,
   Right against the forest fence,
   By St Agnes fountain.'

3. 'Bring me flesh and bring me wine,
   Bring me pine logs hither:
   Thou and I will see him dine,
   When we bear them thither.'
   Page and monarch, forth they went,
   Forth they went together;
   Through the rude wind's wild lament
   And the bitter weather.

4. 'Sire, the night is darker now,
   And the wind blows stronger;
   Fails my heart, I know not how;
   I can go no longer.'
   'Mark my footsteps, good my page;
   Tread thou in them boldly:
   Thou shalt find the winter's rage
   Freeze thy blood less coldly.'

5. In his master's steps he trod,
   Where the snow lay dinted;
   Heat was in the very sod
   Which the saint had printed.
   Therefore, Christian men, be sure,
   Wealth or rank possessing,
   You who now will bless the poor,
   Shall yourselves find blessing.

While Shepherds Watched

2. 'Fear not,' said he: for mighty dread
   Had seized their troubled mind;
   'Glad tidings of great joy I bring
   To you and all mankind.'

3. 'To you in David's town this day
   Is born of David's line
   A Saviour, who is Christ the Lord;
   And this shall be the sign:'

4. 'The heavenly Babe you there shall find
   To human view displayed,
   All meanly wrapped in swathing bands,
   And in a manger laid.'

5. Thus spake the seraph; and forthwith
   Appeared a shining throng
   Of angels praising God, who thus
   Addressed their joyful song:

6. 'All glory be to God on high,
   And to the earth be peace;
   Good will henceforth from heaven to men
   Begin and never cease.'

Christmas Carols

Silent Night

1. Si - lent night, Ho - ly

night, All is calm,

all is bright; Round the

Vir - gin Mo - ther and Child,

Ho - ly in - fant so ten - der and

mild,   Sleep   in   hea - ven - ly

peace, _____   Sleep_   in

hea - ven - ly   peace. _____

2. Silent night, Holy night,
   Shepherds quake at the sight;
   Glories stream from heaven afar,
   Heavenly hosts sing Alleluya:
   Christ the Saviour is born,
   Christ the Saviour is born.

3. Silent night, Holy night,
   Son of God, love's pure light;
   Radiance beams from thy holy face,
   With the dawn of redeeming grace;
   Jesus, Lord, at thy birth,
   Jesus, Lord, at thy birth.

Christmas Carols

Away in a Manger

1. A - way in a__ man - ger, no__

crib for a bed, The___

lit - tle Lord Je - sus laid__

down his sweet head. The

stars in the__ bright sky looked

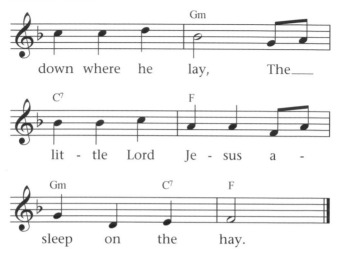

down where he lay,   The___

lit - tle Lord Je - sus a -

sleep   on   the   hay.

2. The cattle are lowing, the Baby awakes,
   But little Lord Jesus, no crying he makes.
   I love thee, Lord Jesus, look down from the sky,
   And stay by my side till morning is nigh.

3. Be near me, Lord Jesus; I ask thee to stay
   Close by me for ever, and love me, I pray.
   Bless all the dear children in thy tender care,
   And fit us for heaven to live with thee there.

Christmas Carols

The First Nowell

1. The_ first___ No - well the_ An - gel did say, Was to cer-tain poor shep - herds in fields as they lay; In_ fields_ where they lay_ keep-ing their sheep, On a cold win-ter's night_ that was_ so deep:

CHORUS

No - well,___ No - well, No - -well, No - well, Born is the King___ of Is - ra - el.

2. They lookèd up and saw a star,
   Shining in the east, beyond them far,
   And to the earth it gave great light,
   And so it continued both day and night:
   Nowell, Nowell, Nowell, Nowell,
   Born is the King of Israel.

3. And by the light of that same star,
   Three wise men came from country far;
   To seek for a King was their intent,
   And to follow the star wherever it went:
   Nowell, Nowell, Nowell, Nowell,
   Born is the King of Israel.

4. This star drew nigh to the north-west,
   O'er Bethlehem it took its rest,
   And there it did both stop and stay,
   Right over the place where Jesus lay:
   Nowell, Nowell, Nowell, Nowell,
   Born is the King of Israel.

5. Then entered in those Wise Men three,
   Full reverently upon their knee,
   And offered there in his presence,
   Their gold and myrrh, and frankincense.
   Nowell, Nowell, Nowell, Nowell,
   Born is the King of Israel.

6. Then let us all with one accord,
   Sing praises to our Heavenly Lord,
   That hath made heaven and earth of nought,
   And with his blood mankind hath bought:
   Nowell, Nowell, Nowell, Nowell,
   Born is the King of Israel.

Once in Royal David's City

2. He came down to earth from heaven
   Who is God and Lord of all,
   And his shelter was a stable,
   And his cradle was a stall;
   With the poor and mean and lowly
   Lived on earth our Saviour holy.

3. And through all his wondrous childhood
   He would honour and obey,
   Love and watch the lowly maiden,
   In whose gentle arms he lay;
   Christian children all must be
   Mild, obedient, good as he.

4. For he is our childhood's pattern,
   Day by day like us he grew,
   He was little, weak, and helpless,
   Tears and smiles like us he knew;
   And he feeleth for our sadness,
   And he shareth in our gladness.

5. And our eyes at last shall see him,
   Through his own redeeming love,
   For that child so dear and gentle
   Is our Lord in heaven above;
   And he leads his children on
   To the place where he is gone.

6. Not in that poor lowly stable,
   With the oxen standing by,
   We shall see him, but in heaven,
   Set at God's right hand on high;
   When like stars his children crowned
   All in white shall wait around.

Ding Dong Merrily on High

1. Ding dong mer-ri-ly on high! In heav'n the bells are ring - ing. Ding dong ve-ri-ly the sky Is riv'n with an-gels sing - ing:

CHORUS

Glo - - - -

- - - - -

- - - ri - a, Ho -

- san - na in ex - cel - sis!

Glo - - - -

- - - - -

Christmas Carols

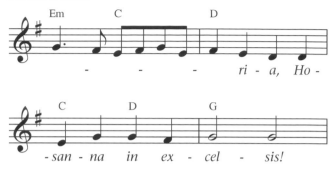

- - - *ri - a, Ho -*

- san - na in ex - cel - sis!

2. E'en so here below, below
   Let steeple bells be swungen.
   And io, io, io
   By priest and people sungen:
   Gloria, Hosanna in excelsis!
   Gloria, Hosanna in excelsis!

3. Pray you, dutifully prime
   Your matin chime, ye ringers;
   May you beautifully rime
   Your evetime song, ye singers:
   Gloria, Hosanna in excelsis!
   Gloria, Hosanna in excelsis!

Deck the Hall

1. Deck the hall with boughs of hol - ly,

Fa la la la la, la la la la,

'Tis the sea - son to be jol - ly,

Fa la la la la, la la la la.

Don we now our gay ap - par - el,

Fa la la, la la la, la la la,

Sing the an-cient Yule-tide ca-rol,

Fa la la la la, la la la la.

2. See the blazing Yule before us,
    Fa la la la la, la la la la,
  Strike the harp and join the chorus,
    Fa la la la la, la la la la.
  Follow me in merry measure,
    Fa la la la la, la la la la,
  While I tell of Yule-tide treasure,
    Fa la la la la, la la la la.

3. Fast away the old year passes,
  Fa la la la la, la la la la,
 Hail the new, you lads and lasses,
  Fa la la la la, la la la la.
 Sing we joyous all together,
  Fa la la la la, la la la la,
 Heedless of the wind and weather,
  Fa la la la la, la la la la.

Jingle Bells

Dash-ing through the snow, In a one-horse o-pen sleigh, O'er the fields we go, Laugh-ing all the way; Bells on bob-tail ring,

Christmas Carols

one - horse   o - pen   sleigh.

Hark! the Herald Angels Sing

1. Hark! the he - rald an - gels sing__

Glo - ry to the new-born King,

Peace on earth and mer - cy mild,_

God and sin - ners re - con - ciled.

Joy - ful all ye na - tions rise,__

Join the tri-umph of the skies;—

With th'an-gel - ic host pro - claim:

'Christ is—— born in Beth - le - hem'.

Hark! the he - rald an - gels sing

Glo - ry—— to the new-born King.

2. Christ, by highest Heav'n adored,
   Christ, the Everlasting Lord,
   Late in time behold him come,
   Offspring of a virgin's womb.
   Veiled in flesh the Godhead see,
   Hail the incarnate Deity!
   Pleased as Man with man to dwell,
   Jesus, our Emmanuel.
   Hark! the herald angels sing
   Glory to the new-born King.

3. Hail, the heaven-born Prince of Peace!
   Hail, the Sun of Righteousness!
   Light and life to all he brings,
   Risen with healing in his wings.
   Mild he lays his glory by,
   Born that man no more may die,
   Born to raise the sons of earth,
   Born to give them second birth.
   Hark! the herald angels sing
   Glory to the new-born King.

We Three Kings

1. We three kings of Or - i - ent are;

Bear - ing gifts we trav - erse a - far;

Field and foun - tain, moor and moun - tain,

Fol - low - ing yon - der star;

CHORUS

O_____ star of won - der, star of night,

Star with roy - al beau - ty bright,

West-ward lead - ing still pro-ceed - ing,

Guide us to thy per - fect light.

2. *Melchior:*
   Born a king on Bethlehem plain,
   Gold I bring, to crown him again –
   King for ever, ceasing never,
   Over us all to reign:
       O star of wonder, star of night,
       Star with royal beauty bright,
       Westward leading still proceeding,
       Guide us to thy perfect light.

3. *Caspar:*
   Frankincense to offer have I;
   Incense owns a Deity nigh:
   Prayer and praising, all men raising,
   Worship him, God most high:
   > *O star of wonder, star of night,*
   > *Star with royal beauty bright,*
   > *Westward leading still proceeding,*
   > *Guide us to thy perfect light.*

4. *Balthazar:*
   Myrrh is mine; its bitter perfume
   Breathes a life of gathering gloom,
   Sorrowing, sighing, bleeding, dying,
   Sealed in the stone-cold tomb:
   > *O star of wonder, star of night,*
   > *Star with royal beauty bright,*
   > *Westward leading still proceeding,*
   > *Guide us to thy perfect light.*

5. Glorious now, behold him arise;
   King, and God, and sacrifice.
   Heaven sings alleluya,
   Alleluya the earth replies:
   > *O star of wonder, star of night,*
   > *Star with royal beauty bright,*
   > *Westward leading still proceeding,*
   > *Guide us to thy perfect light.*

The Little Drummer Boy

1. 'Come', they told me, Pa-

-rum-pa-pum - pum, _____

'Our new-born King to see! Pa-

-rum-pa-pum - pum, _____

Our fin - est gifts we bring, Pa-

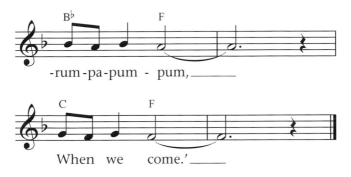

-rum-pa-pum - pum,_____

When we come.'_____

2. 'Little Baby, Pa-rum-pa-pum-pum,
   I am a poor boy too, Pa-rum-pa-pum-pum,
   I have no gift to bring, Pa-rum-pa-pum-pum,
   That's fit to give our King! Pa-rum-pa-pum-pum,
   Rum-pa-pum-pum, rum-pa-pum-pum,
   Shall I play for You, Pa-rum-pa-pum-pum,
   On my drum?'

3. Mary nodded, Pa-rum-pa-pum-pum,
   The ox and lamb kept time, Pa-rum-pa-pum-pum,
   I played my drum for Him, Pa-rum-pa-pum-pum,
   I played my best for Him, Pa-rum-pa-pum-pum,
   Rum-pa-pum-pum, rum-pa-pum-pum,
   Then He smiled at me, Pa-rum-pa-pum-pum,
   Me and my drum!

Christmas Carols

Little Donkey

Don't give up now, lit-tle don - key,

Beth - le-hem's in sight.

CHORUS

Ring out those bells to - night,

Beth - le - hem, Beth - le - hem.

Fol - low that star to - night,

Beth - le - hem, Beth - le - hem.

Lit - tle don - key, lit - tle don - key,

Had a hea - vy day.

Lit - tle don - key, car - ry Ma - ry

safe - ly on her way.

2. Little donkey, little donkey,
   On the dusty road.
   There are wise men, waiting for a
   Sign to bring them here.
   Do not falter, little donkey,
   There's a star ahead.
   It will guide you, little donkey,
   To a cattle shed.

   Ring out those bells tonight,
   Bethlehem, Bethlehem.
   Follow that star tonight,
   Bethlehem, Bethlehem.
   Little donkey, little donkey,
   Had a heavy day.
   Little donkey, carry Mary
   Safely on her way.

The Three Drovers

1. A - cross the plains___ one

Christ-mas night, Three dro-vers rid - ing

blythe___ and gay,___ Looked

up and saw a star - ry light, More

rad - iant than the Mil - ky Way; And

on   their hearts such won - der fell, they

sang with joy, 'No - el,__ No - el,__ No-

-el,__ No - el,__ No - el.'____

2. The black swans flew across the sky,
   The wild dog called across the plain,
   The starry lustre blazed on high,
   Still echoed on the Heavenly strain;
   And still they sang, 'Noel! Noel!'
   Those drovers three, 'Noel! Noel!
   Noel! Noel! Noel!'

3. The air was dry with Summer heat
   And smoke was on the yellow Moon;
   But from the Heavens, faint and sweet,
   Came floating down a wond'rous tune
   And as they heard, they sang full well,
   Those drovers three, 'Noel! Noel!
   Noel! Noel! Noel!'

See, Amid the Winter's Snow

1. See, a-mid the win-ter's snow,

Born for us on earth be-low,

See, the ten-der lamb ap-pears,

Pro-mised from e-ter-nal years!

CHORUS

Hail, thou e-ver bless-ed morn!

Hail,   Re - demp -tions's   hap - py   dawn!

Sing through all   Je - ru - sa - lem,

Christ   is born   in   Beth - le - hem!

2. Lo, within a manger lies
   He who built the starry skies,
   He who, throned in height sublime,
   Sits amid the cherubim!
   Hail, thou ever blessed morn!
   Hail, Redemption's happy dawn!
   Sing through all Jerusalem,
   Christ is born in Bethlehem!

3. Say, ye holy shepherds, say,
   What your joyful news today;
   Wherefore have ye left your sheep
   On the lonely mountain steep?
   Hail, thou ever blessed morn!
   Hail, Redemption's happy dawn!
   Sing through all Jerusalem,
   Christ is born in Bethlehem!

4. 'As we watched at dead at night,
   Lo, we saw a wondrous light;
   Angels singing "Peace on earth"
   Told us of the Saviour's birth.'
   Hail, thou ever blessed morn!
   Hail, Redemption's happy dawn!
   Sing through all Jerusalem,
   Christ is born in Bethlehem!

5. Sacred infant, all divine,
   What a tender love was Thine,
   Thus to come from highest bliss
   Down to such a world as this!
   Hail, thou ever blessed morn!
   Hail, Redemption's happy dawn!
   Sing through all Jerusalem,
   Christ is born in Bethlehem!

6. Teach, O teach us, holy child,
   By Thy face so meek and mild,
   Teach us to resemble Thee
   In Thy sweet humility.
   Hail, thou ever blessed morn!
   Hail, Redemption's happy dawn!
   Sing through all Jerusalem,
   Christ is born in Bethlehem!

The Holly and the Ivy

1. The hol-ly and the i - vy, When they are both full grown, Of___ all the trees that are in the wood, The_ hol - ly bears the crown.

CHORUS

O The ris - ing of the sun___ And the

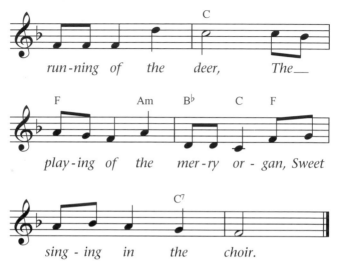

run-ning of the deer, The__

play-ing of the mer-ry or-gan, Sweet

sing - ing in the choir.

2. The holly bears a blossom,
   As white as the lily flower,
   And Mary bore sweet Jesus Christ
   To be our sweet Saviour:
       O The rising of the sun
       And the running of the deer,
       The playing of the merry organ,
       Sweet singing in the choir.

3. The holly bears a berry,
    As red as any blood,
    And Mary bore sweet Jesus Christ
    To do poor sinners good:
        O The rising of the sun
        And the running of the deer,
        The playing of the merry organ,
        Sweet singing in the choir.

4. The holly bears a prickle,
    As sharp as any thorn,
    And Mary bore sweet Jesus Christ
    On Christmas day in the morn:
        O The rising of the sun
        And the running of the deer,
        The playing of the merry organ,
        Sweet singing in the choir.

5. The holly bears a bark,
    As bitter as any gall,
    And Mary bore sweet Jesus Christ
    For to redeem us all:
        O The rising of the sun
        And the running of the deer,
        The playing of the merry organ,
        Sweet singing in the choir.

6. The holly and the ivy,
    When they are both full grown,
    Of all the trees that are in the wood,
    The holly bears the crown:
        O The rising of the sun
        And the running of the deer,
        The playing of the merry organ,
        Sweet singing in the choir.

I Saw Three Ships

1. I saw three ships come sail-ing in, On Christ-mas Day, on Christ-mas Day, I saw three ships come sail - ing in On Christ-mas Day in the morn - ing.

2. And what was in those ships all three?
   On Christmas Day, on Christmas Day,
   I saw three ships come sailing in
   On Christmas day in the morning.

3. Our Saviour Christ and his lady.
   On Christmas Day, on Christmas Day,
   I saw three ships come sailing in
   On Christmas day in the morning.

4. Pray, whither sailed those ships all three?
   On Christmas Day, on Christmas Day,
   I saw three ships come sailing in
   On Christmas day in the morning.

5. O, they sailed into Bethlehem.
   On Christmas Day, on Christmas Day,
   I saw three ships come sailing in
   On Christmas day in the morning.

6. And all the bells on earth shall ring.
   On Christmas Day, on Christmas Day,
   I saw three ships come sailing in
   On Christmas day in the morning.

7. And all the angels in Heaven shall sing.
   On Christmas Day, on Christmas Day,
   I saw three ships come sailing in
   On Christmas day in the morning.

8. And all the souls on earth shall sing.
   On Christmas Day, on Christmas Day,
   I saw three ships come sailing in
   On Christmas day in the morning.

9. Then let us all rejoice amain!
   On Christmas Day, on Christmas Day,
   I saw three ships come sailing in
   On Christmas day in the morning.

O Come, All Ye Faithful

1. O come, all ye faith - ful,

Joy - ful and tri - um - phant. O

come ye, O come_ ye to

Beth - le - hem;

Come and be - hold him

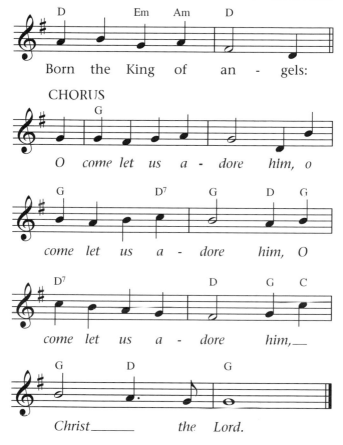

Christmas Carols

2. God of God,
   Light of Light,
   Lo, he abhors not the Virgin's womb;
   Very God,
   Begotten not created:
   O come let us adore him,
   O come let us adore him,
   O come let us adore him,
   Christ the Lord.

3. Sing choirs of angels,
   Sing in exultation,
   Sing, all ye citizens of heaven above;
   Glory to God
   In the highest:
   O come let us adore him,
   O come let us adore him,
   O come let us adore him,
   Christ the Lord.

4. Yea, Lord, we greet thee,
   Born this happy morning.
   Jesu, to thee be glory given;
   Word of the Father,
   Now in flesh appearing:
   > *O come let us adore him,*
   > *O come let us adore him,*
   > *O come let us adore him,*
   > *Christ the Lord.*

God Rest You Merry Gentlemen

1. God rest you mer-ry gen-tle-men, Let
no - thing you dis - may. Re -
-mem-ber Christ our Sa - viour Was
born on Christ-mas day, To
save our souls from Sa-tan's power When

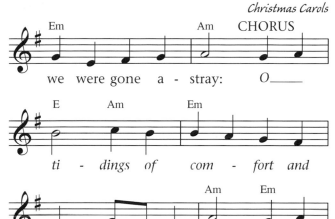

we were gone a - stray: O____

ti - dings of com - fort and

joy, Com - fort and joy, O____

ti - dings of com - fort and joy.

2. In Bethlehem in Jewry
   This blessed Babe was born,
   And laid within a manger
   Upon this blessed morn,
   The which his Mother Mary
   Did nothing take in scorn:
   > *O tidings of comfort and joy,*
   > *Comfort and joy,*
   > *O tidings of comfort and joy.*

3. From God our heavenly Father
   A blessed angel came,
   And unto certain shepherds
   Brought tidings of the same,
   How that in Bethlehem was born
   The son of God by name:
   > *O tidings of comfort and joy,*
   > *Comfort and joy,*
   > *O tidings of comfort and joy.*

4. 'Fear not' then said the angel,
   'Let nothing you affright;
   This day is born a Saviour
   Unto a Virgin bright
   To free all you who trust in him
   From Satan's power and might':
       O tidings of comfort and joy,
       Comfort and joy,
       O tidings of comfort and joy.

5. The shepherds at these tidings
   Rejoicèd much in mind,
   And left their flocks a-feeding
   In tempest, storm, and wind,
   And went to Bethlehem straightway
   The Son of God to find:
       O tidings of comfort and joy,
       Comfort and joy,
       O tidings of comfort and joy.

6. Now when they came to Bethlehem
   Whereat the Infant lay,
   They found him in a manger
   Where oxen feed on hay;
   His Mother Mary kneeling down
   Unto the Lord did pray:
   > *O tidings of comfort and joy,*
   > *Comfort and joy,*
   > *O tidings of comfort and joy.*

7. Now to the Lord sing praises
   All you within this place,
   And with true love and brotherhood
   Each other now embrace;
   This holy tide of Christmas
   All others doth deface:
   > *O tidings of comfort and joy,*
   > *Comfort and joy,*
   > *O tidings of comfort and joy.*

O Little Town of Bethlehem

1. O lit-tle town of Beth-le-hem, How still we__ see thee lie! A- bove thy deep and dream-less_sleep The si - lent_ stars go by: Yet__ in thy dark streets shi - neth The

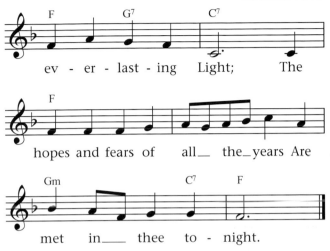

ev - er - last - ing Light; The

hopes and fears of all__ the_years Are

met in__ thee to - night.

2. For Christ is born of Mary;
   And, gathered all above,
   While mortals sleep, the angels keep
   Their watch of wondering love.
   O, morning stars, together
   Proclaim the holy birth,
   And praises sing to God the King
   And peace to men on earth.

3. How silently, how silently,
   The wondrous gift is given!
   So God imparts to human hearts
   The blessings of his heaven.
   No ear may hear his coming;
   But in this world of sin,
   Where meek souls will receive him, still
   The dear Christ enters in.

4. O holy Child of Bethlehem,
   Descend to us, we pray;
   Cast out our sins, and enter in:
   Be born in us today.
   We hear the Christmas angels
   The great glad tidings tell:
   O come to us, abide with us,
   Our Lord Emmanuel.

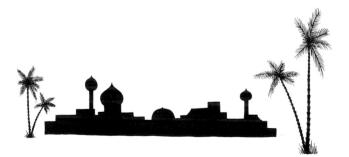

The Truth About Christmas

PHILIP ARDAGH

The traditions of Christmas unravelled!

Have you ever wondered:

Who decided to celebrate Christ's birthday on
25th December?

Why we kiss under the mistletoe?

Where the flying reindeer came from?

What all the holly and ivy is for?

Why Christmas pudding
is Christmas pudding shaped?

The answers to these and many other
festive questions are packed within the
covers of this book.

Christmas Poems

CHOSEN BY GABY MORGAN

A wonderful anthology of both classic and brand-new poems, carols and hymns for Christmas. It captures all the emotion and enjoyment of the festive season, from anticipation to happiness, to the joy of the New Year.

REINDEER REPORT

Chimneys: colder.
Flightpaths: busier.
Driver: Christmas (F)
Still baffled by postcodes.

Children: more
And stay up later.
Presents: heavier
Pay: frozen.

Mission in spite
Of all this
Accomplished.

U.A.Thanthorpe.